THE VERY BEST

Produced by
Alfred Music
P.O. Box 10003
Van Nuys, CA 91410-0003
alfred.com

Printed in USA.

ISBN-10: 1-4706-1704-8
ISBN-13: 978-1-4706-1704-2

Cover photo: © Doors Property, LLC. Photography by Paul Ferrara.

THE VERY BEST OF

CONTENTS

BACK DOOR MAN

Words and Music by
WILLIE DIXON

Moderate blues-rock ♩ = 92

Wha! Yuh!

C'mon, yeah, yeah.

C'mon,

Verse 2:

8

Verse 3:

3. You men eat your din - ner, eat your pork and beans,

I eat more chick-en an - y man ev - er seen, yeah, yeah.

THE CHANGELING

Words and Music by
THE DOORS

The Changeling - 9 - 1

Verse 1:

I had mon-ey,

I had none.___ I had

mon-ey, I had none.___

N.C.

But I nev-er been so broke that I could-n't leave

Verse 2:

mon - ey,_____ yeah, and I had none.__

N.C.

But I nev - er been so broke that I could-n't leave town._____

Guitar solo:

B♭5

BREAK ON THROUGH
(To the Other Side)

Words and Music by
THE DOORS

Moderately bright ♩ = 182

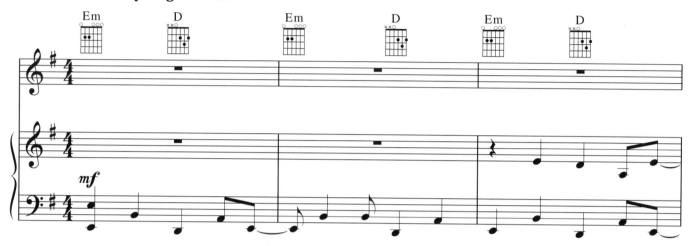

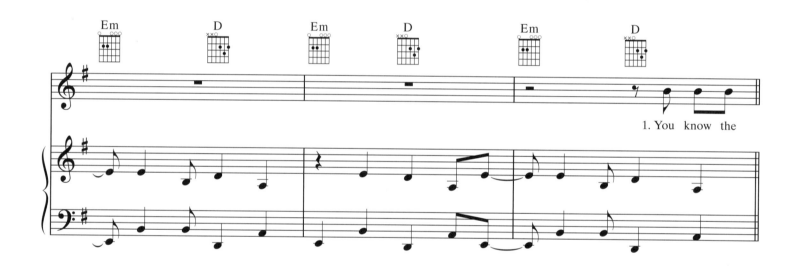

1. You know the

Verse 1:

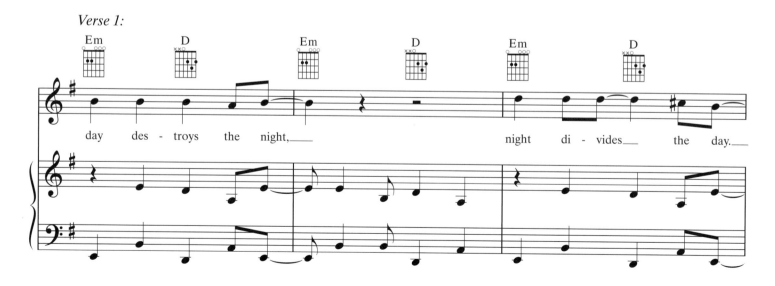

day des-troys the night,___ night di-vides___ the day.___

Break on Through - 8 - 1

Verse 2:

Organ solo:

Ev - 'ry - bod - y____ loves my ba - by.____

24

Verse 3:

Verse 4:

4. Made the scene,___ *from* week to week,___ day to day,___

hour to hour.___ Gate is straight,___ deep and wide...___

Break on through_ to the oth - er side._ Break on through_ to the

oth - er side._ Break on through._ Break on through._

Break on through._ Break on through._ Yeah, yeah, yeah, yeah,

yeah, yeah, yeah, yeah, yeah.

THE CRYSTAL SHIP

Words and Music by
THE DOORS

Verse 3:

tell me where___ your free - dom lies;___ the streets are fields___ that

nev - er die.___ De - liv - er me from

rea - sons why you'd rath - er cry,___ I'd rath - er fly.___

3. Oh,

Verse 4:

4. The crys - tal ship___ is be - ing___ filled,_ a thou-sand girls,_ a thou-sand thrills,_ a mil lion ways to spend your time. When we get back,___ I'll___ drop a line.___

rit.

END OF THE NIGHT

Words and Music by
JIM MORRISON

Moderately slow ♩ = 73

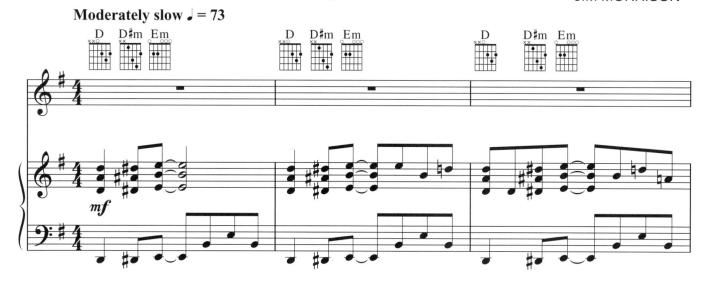

Take the high-way to the end of the night,_

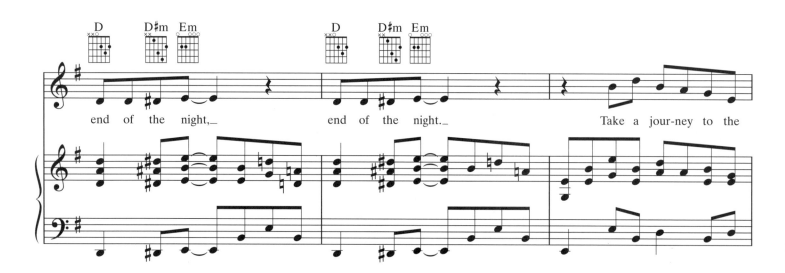

end of the night,_   end of the night._   Take a jour-ney to the

End of the Night - 4 - 1

end of the night,_ end of the night,_ end of the night._

(Guitar solo ad lib....

...end solo)

End of the Night - 4 - 4

THE END

Gtr. in Dbl. Drop D tuning:
⑥ = D   ③ = G
⑤ = A   ② = B
④ = D   ①= D

Words and Music by
THE DOORS

Moderately ♩ = 112

(with pedal)

Chorus:

This is the end,　　beau - ti - ful　friend.＿

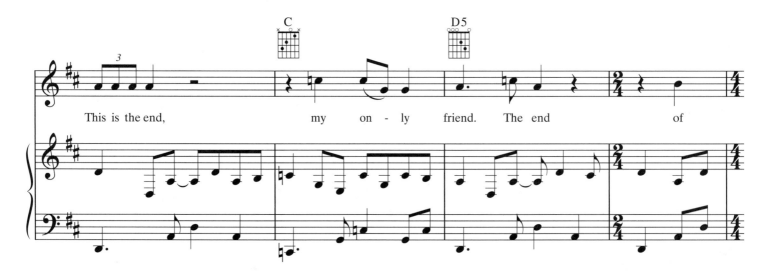

This is the end,　　my　on - ly　friend.　The　end　　of

The End - 13 - 1

Bridge:

1.2.3.

Instrumental:

(Guitar solo ad lib.)

4.

Verse 1:

1. Lost in a___ Ro-man wil - der - ness of pain.___

And all the chil - dren are in -

40

2. There's

Verses 2, 3 & 4:

___ dan-ger___ on the edge of ___ town._
3.4. *See additional lyrics*

Ride the king's high - way, ba - by.

Weird scenes in - side___ the gold__ mine.

44

I want to... love____ you, yeah.__ Come on, yeah!__

Verse 5:

Faster ♩ = 124

Instrumental:

Repeat as desired for solo

Freely

The end of laugh-ter and soft___ lies.___

The end of nights we tried to

die. This is the end.____

rit.

D

Verse 3:
The West is the best.
The West is the best.
Get here and we'll do the rest.
The blue bus is callin' us.
The blue bus is callin' us.
Driver, where you takin' us?

Verse 4:
Spoken:
The killer awoke before dawn, he put his boots on.
He took a face from the ancient gallery and he walked on down the hall.
He went into the room where his sister lived, and... then he paid a visit to his brother,
And then he... he walked on down the hall, yeah, and he came to a door... and he looked inside.
"Father," "Yes, son," "I want to kill you."
Mother, I want to... love you, yeah. Come on, yeah!

FIVE TO ONE

Words and Music by
THE DOORS

Moderately ♩ = 92

Verse 1:

1. Five to one,__ ba - by,__ one in five._____ No one here_____ gets__

out a - live,__ now. You get yours,____ ba - by, I'll get mine.____

Gon - na make it, ba - by, if we try.____

Am

Verse 2:

2. The old___ get old___ and the young get strong - er.

May take a week___ and it may take long - er.___ They got the guns___ but,___

N.C.

we got the num - bers.___ Gon - na win,___ yeah, we're tak - in' o - ver.

Come on!

Guitar solo:

Verse 3:

3. Your ball-room days are o-ver, ba-by, night__ is draw-ing near.__

Shad-ows__ of the eve-ning_____ crawl a-cross the years.__

52

Five to One - 7 - 4

Guitar Solo 2:

(lead vocal ad lib.)

Five to One - 7 - 5

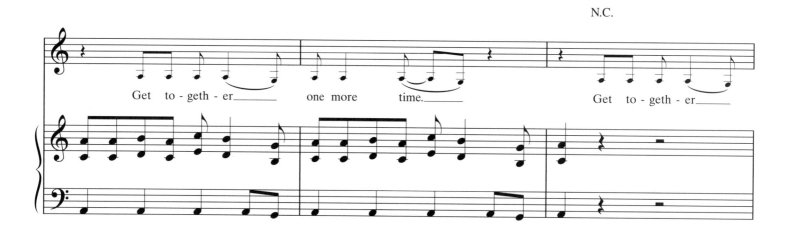

Spoken: "Hey, come on honey, you go along home and wait for me, baby. I'll be here in just a little while.

You see, I got to go out in this car with these people and get..."

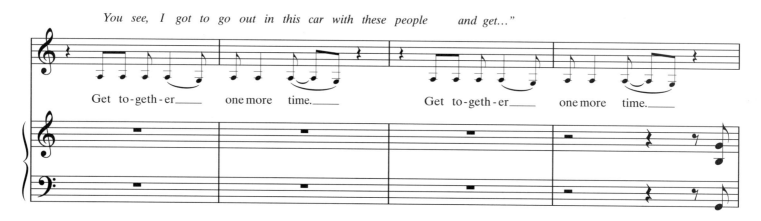

Repeat ad lib. and fade

GLORIA

Words and Music by
VAN MORRISON

Moderately fast rock ♩ = 126

58

at just a - bout mid - night.___ She make me feel so good,_

make me feel al - right._____

She come 'round my street,_

___ now. She come to my house___ and

Gloria - 14 - 3

Spoken: Hey! What's your name? How old are you? Where'd you go to school? Uh huh. Yeah? Uh huh. Yeah. Oh? Oh. Yeah. Oh yeah.
Oh yeah. Mmm. Well, now that we know each other a little bit better, why don't you come over here...

Chorus:

Make me feel al - right! Glo - ri - a!

Verse 2:

2. You were my queen and I was your fool,_____ rid - ing home_ af -

ter school._

You took me home_____

64

to your house.___

Your fa - ther's at work.___

___ Your ma - ma's out shop - ping___ a - round.___

___ Checked me in - to your room,___

___ showed me your thing.___ Why'd you

do it, ba - by?   Uh,___ get-ting

soft - er,_____ slow it down._____ Uh,

rit. e dim poco a poco

___ Soft - er,_____   get it down._____

Now, you show me your

thing.

Spoken: Eee yeah!

New Slower Tempo ♩ = 100

Spoken: Wrap your legs around my neck.

Wrap your arms around my feet. Yeah.

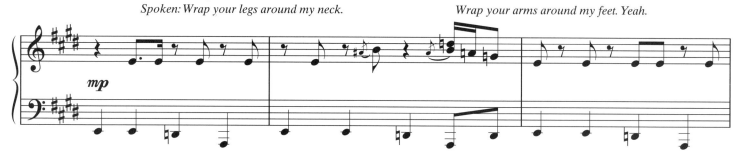

Wrap your hair around my skin. Yeah.

I'm gonna...huh alright. Okay. Yeah.

It's gettin' harder. It's gettin' too darn fast. Yeah.

accel.

It's gettin' harder. Alright.

Come on, love, now let's get it on!

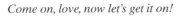

Too late! Too late! Too late! Too late! Too late! Too late!

Tempo One ♩ = 126

Can't stop! Oh!

Make me feel al - right!

Shuffle ♩ = 126 (♫ = ♪³♪)

Spoken: Keep the whole thing goin', man. Alright!

Alright!

HELLO, I LOVE YOU

Words and Music by
THE DOORS

Moderately ♩ = 120

Chorus:

Hel - lo, I love you, won't you

tell me your name?___ Hel - lo, I love you, let me

Hello, I Love You - 6 - 1

Verse 3:

3. Side - walk crouch - es___ at her feet,___ like a dog___ that begs for

some-thing sweet.___ Do you hope to make her see, you fool?___ Do you

hope to pluck this dusk - y jew - el? Hel - lo! Hel - lo!

Hello, I Love You - 6 - 5

L.A. WOMAN

Words and Music by
THE DOORS

Moderately bright ♩ = 176

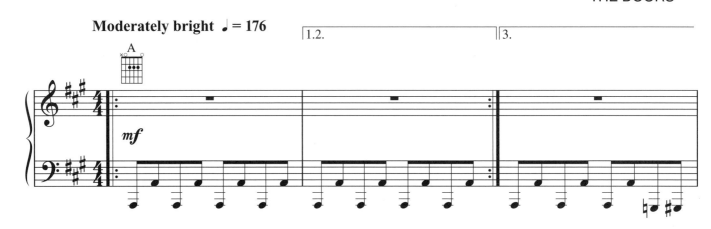

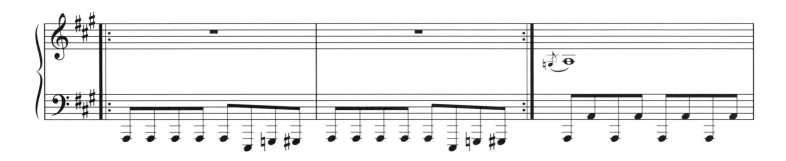

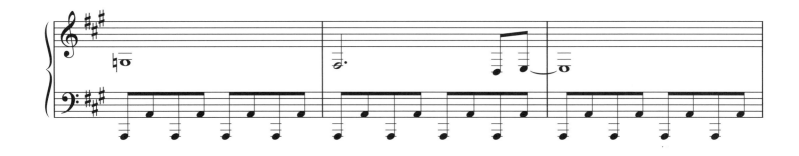

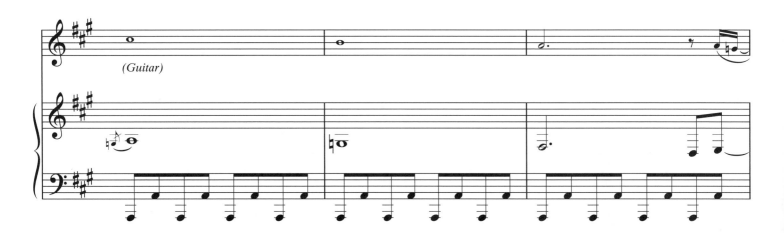

Verse 1:

just got in-to town a-bout an hour a-go.___ *(Guitar)*

I took a look a-round, see which___ way the wind___ blows.

With a lit-tle girl in a

Hol - ly - wood bun - ga - low.___ Are you a

luck - y lit - tle la - dy in the cit - y of light?___

Or just an - oth - er lost an - gel?_____ Cit - y of night,___

G   A

cit - y of night.___

Cit - y of night,___ cit - y of night.

Whoa! Come on!

Guitar solo:

(Inst. solo ad lib....

…end solo)

Chorus:

L. A.___ wom - an,   L. A.___ wom - an.

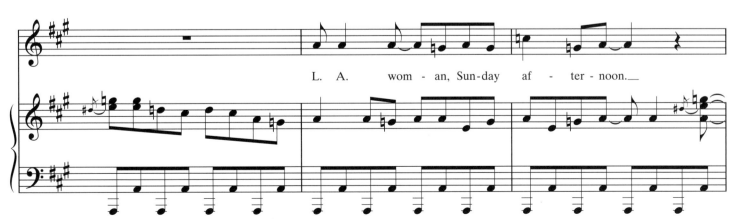

L. A.   wom - an, Sun-day af - ter - noon.___

L.A. Woman - 20 - 6

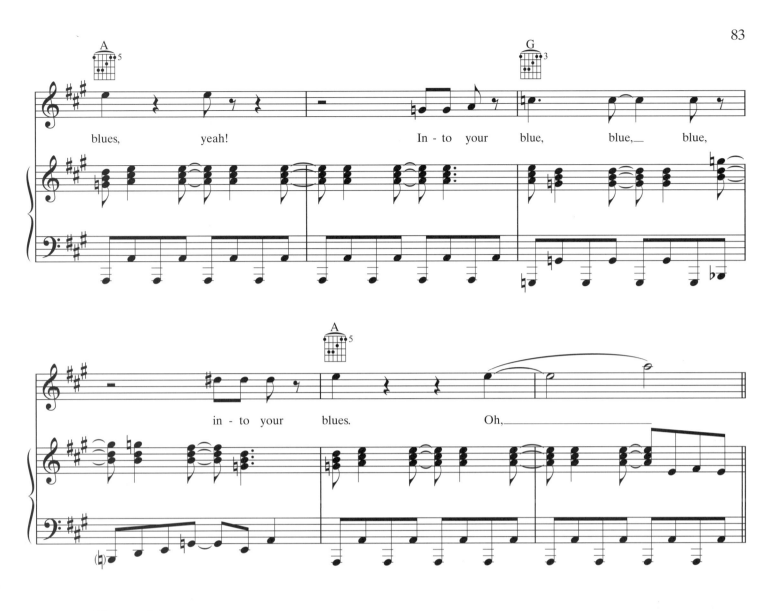

blues,   yeah!   In - to your   blue,   blue,___   blue,

in - to your   blues.   Oh,_____

Piano solo:

yeah.

84

Interlude 1:

(Piano 2)

know they are a li - ar.___

Driv - in' down your free - way,___

mid - night al - leys

roam.

Oh,

yeah.

Verse 2:

2. Well,   just got in - to town a - bout an   hour   a - go.

Took a look a-round me, which way the wind blows.

With a lit-tle girl in a Hol-ly-wood bun - ga-low.

Are you a luck-y lit-tle la-dy in the cit-y of light?

94

Guitar solo:

Come on!__

(*Inst. solo ad lib....*)

Chorus:

Repeat ad lib. and fade

L. A. Wom - an._____

L. A.__ Wom - an._____

LIGHT MY FIRE

Words and Music by
THE DOORS

LOVE HER MADLY

Words and Music by
THE DOORS

Moderately fast ♩ = 144

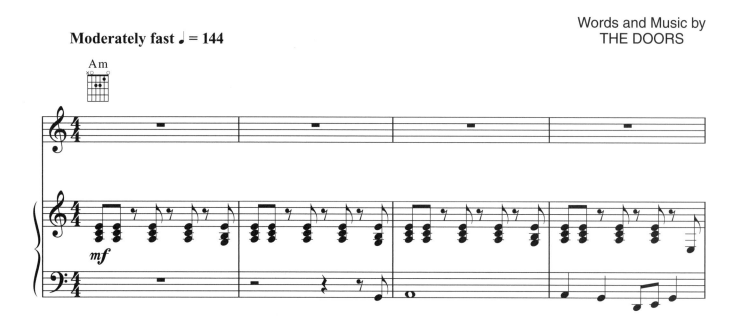

Verse:

Love Her Madly - 8 - 1

so sing a lone - ly song___ of a

deep blue dream._ Sev - en hors - es___ seem

To Coda ⊕

to be on the mark.

Organ solo:

Instrumental solo:

Well, don't you love her____ mad - ly?_____ Ah, don't you

love her____ mad - ly? Ah, don't you love her____ mad - ly?_____

Repeat ad lib. and fade

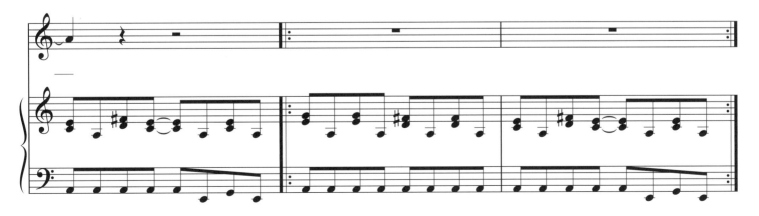

GHOST SONG

Words and Music by
THE DOORS

Moderately ♩ = 120

(with pedal)

Awake.   Shake dreams from your hair, my pretty child,   my sweet one.

Choose the day and choose the sign of your day,   the day's divinity,   First thing you see.

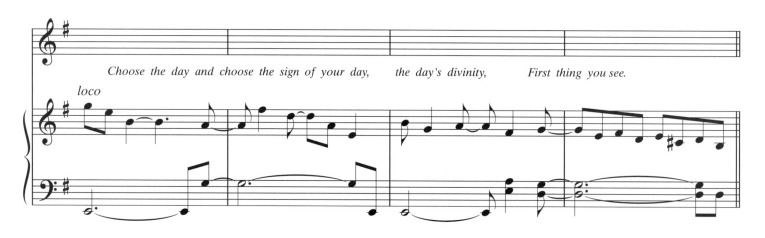

N.C.

Indians scattered, on dawn's highway bleeding, ghosts crowd the young child's fragile eggshell mind.

119

Ghost Song - 7 - 6

When the true king's murderer's are allowed to roam free, a thousand magicians arise in the land.

Where are the feasts we were promised?

LOVE ME TWO TIMES

Words and Music by
THE DOORS

Moderately ♩ = 126 (♫ = ♪³♪)

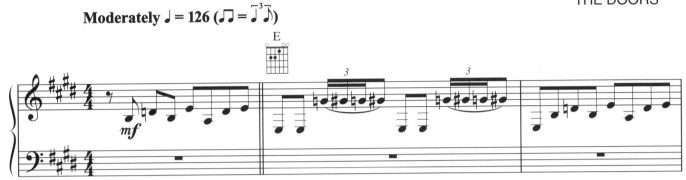

1. Love me two times, ba -

Verse 1:

- by,____ love me twice to - day.____

Love Me Two Times - 9 - 1

Verse 2:

2. Love me one time,   I could not   speak._

A7

Love me one   time,_

E

yeah,   my knees_ gone   weak._   Love me two times,_ girl,_

124

Love Me Two Times - 9 - 4

Keyboard solo:

Verse 3:

3. Love me one time,___

I could not speak.___

Love me one time, ba - by,

LOVE STREET

Words and Music by
THE DOORS

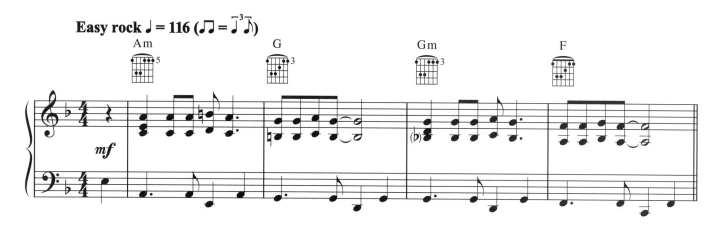

Verse 1:

1. She lives__ on Love Street, lin-gers long_____ on Love Street..

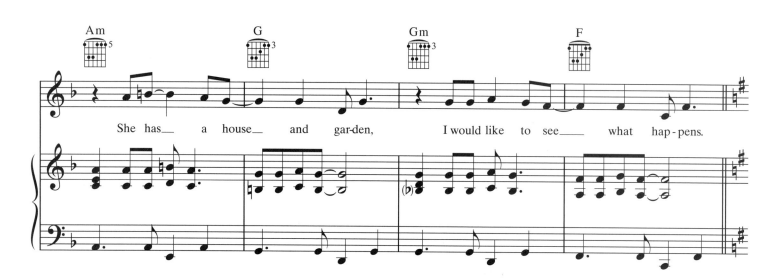

She has__ a house__ and gar-den, I would like to see__ what hap-pens.

Verse 4:

4. She lives_ on Love Street, a - lin-gers long___ on Love Street._

She has__ a house__ and gar - den, I would like to see____ what hap - pens.

Repeat ad lib. and fade

La la__ la, la la la la,___ la la__ la, la la la la.___

MY EYES HAVE SEEN YOU

Words and Music by
THE DOORS

*Harmony 2nd time only.

138

My Eyes Have Seen You - 5 - 4

MOONLIGHT DRIVE

Words and Music by
THE DOORS

Moderate rock ♩ = 115

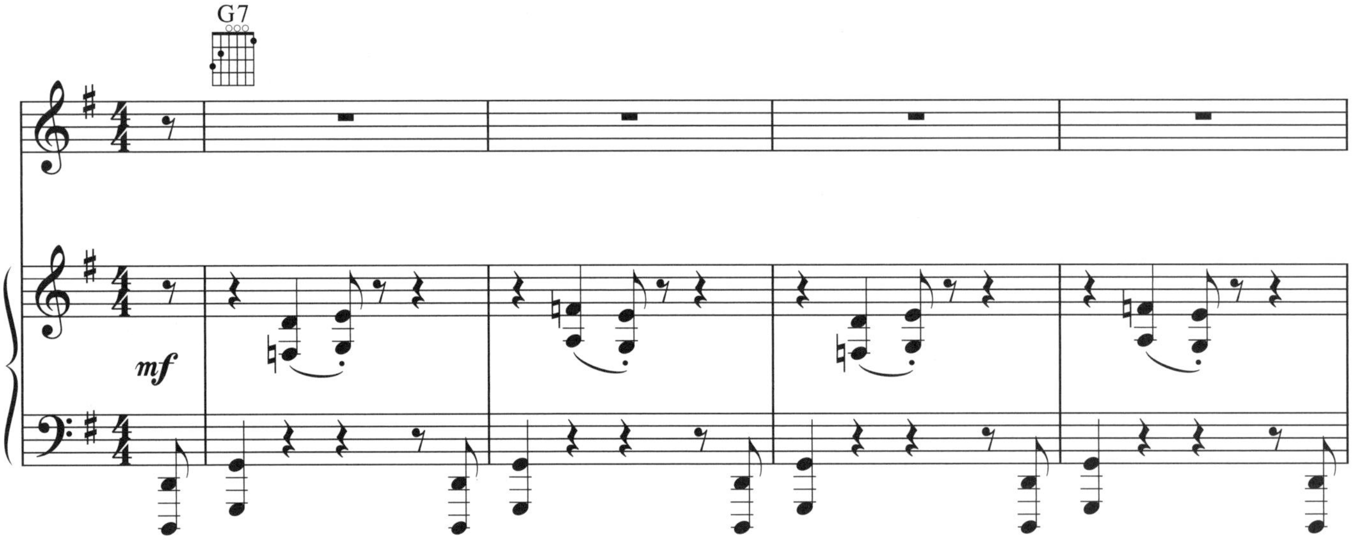
G7
mf

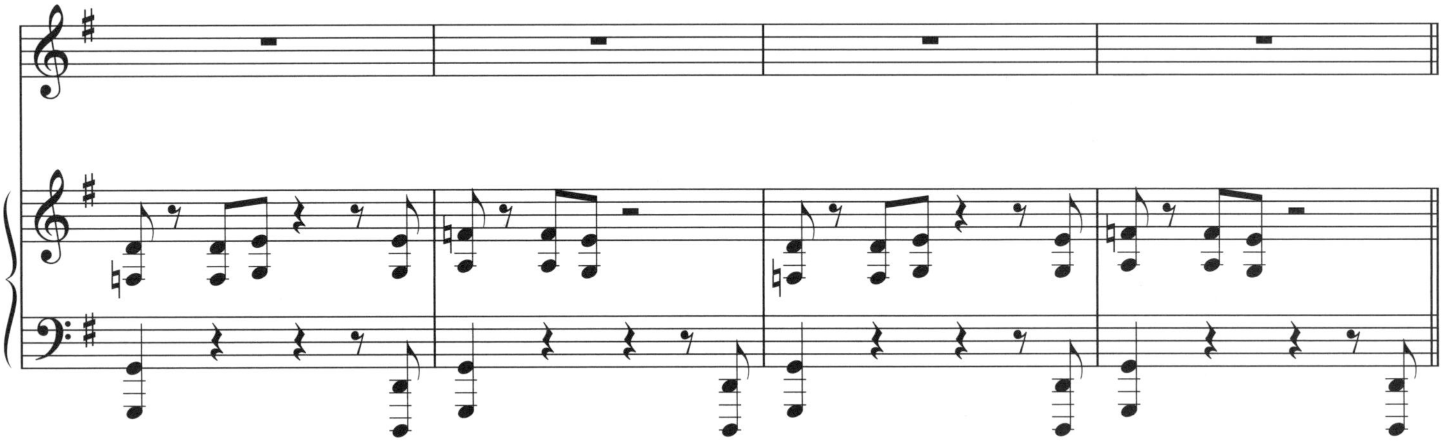

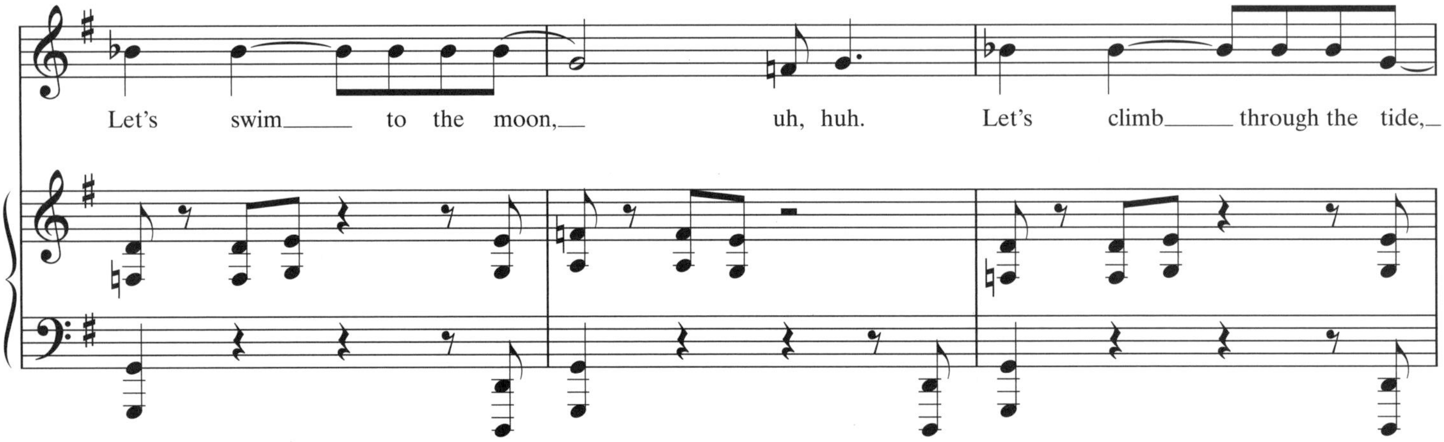
Let's swim___ to the moon,__ uh, huh. Let's climb___ through the tide,__

pen - e - trate __ the eve - nin' __ that __ the

cit - y sleeps to hide. __

D7

Let's swim out __ to - night __

__ love; it's our turn to try, __

G7

parked be - side the o - cean on our moon - light

...end solo)

Let's swim to the moon._____ Let's climb through the tide.__

_____ You reach a hand to hold___ me, but I

can't be your guide._____ Eas - y, I____

NOT TO TOUCH THE EARTH

Words and Music by
THE DOORS

Moderately ♩ = 112

Verse 1:

1. Not to touch the earth, not to see the sun. Noth-ing left to do but run, run,_ run._ Let's run,_

Not to Touch the Earth - 8 - 1

run with me. Let's run.

N.C.

2. The

Verse 2:

man - sion is warm at the top of the hill,___ rich are the rooms and the com-forts there.___

Red are the arms of lux - u - ri - ant chairs___ and you won't know a thing 'til you get in - side.___

Not to Touch the Earth - 8 - 3

Verse 3:

out - laws lived by the side of a lake._ The min-is-ter's daught-er's in love with a snake,_ who

lives in a well by the side of the road._ Wake up girl,_ we're al-most home._ Yeah,

Solos:

c'mon!

Guitar and keyboard solo ad lib....

We should see_ the gates_ by morn - in'.

get you___ soon, soon,_____

soon._____

freely
Fm

F7(♯9)

Spoken: I am the Lizard King. I can do anything.

PEACE FROG

Words and Music by
THE DOORS

Moderate rock ♩ = 112

blood in the street, it's up___ to my an - kles.___

1. There's

2. *See additional lyrics*

(She

Verses 1 & 2:

Peace Frog - 7 - 2

156

She came and then she drove a - way, sun - light in her hair.

(She

Guitar solo:

Interlude:

Spoken: Indians scattered on dawn's highway, bleeding.

Ghosts crowd the young child's fragile eggshell mind.

Verse 3:

3. Blood on the streets in the town of New Ha - ven.

Blood in the streets, it's up___ to my knees.

Blood in the streets in the town___ of Chi-ca-go.___

Blood on the rise, it's fol-low-ing me.___

Verse 2:
(She came) Blood in the streets runs a river of sadness.
(She came) Blood in the streets, it's up to my thigh.
(She came) Yeah, the river runs right down the length of the city.
(She came) The women are crying red rivers of weepin'.

She came into town and then she drove away,
Sunlight in her hair.

ROADHOUSE BLUES

(Live Version)

Words and Music by
THE DOORS

Moderate blues rock ♩ = 121 (♫ = ♩♪)

Roadhouse Blues - 11 - 1

Verse 1:

163

Verse 2:

gon - na have a   real old,_____   a good time.____

2. Yeah,   in   back   of the road - house they got   some_bun - ga - lows.

____   Yeah,   in   back   of the road - house, they

Roadhouse Blues - 11 - 3

You got - ta

dim.   ...end solo)

Bridge:

roll, roll, roll, you got - ta thrill__ my soul, al - right.

Roll, roll, roll, roll - a thrill my soul.__ You got - ta

beep a gunk a chu-cha, honk konk konk.__ You got - ta each you pu - na, each ya

bop a lu - ba, each yall___ bump a ke-chonk, ease sa kunk,__ yeah, ride.__

Save our cit - y,_____ save our cit - y,_____

right now.

3. And, I

Verse 3:

woke up this morn - ing, I got____ my - self a beer.____

Chorus:

PEOPLE ARE STRANGE

Words and Music by
THE DOORS

Chorus:

strange, ... fac - es come out___ of the rain,___ when you're strange.__

___ No one re - mem - bers your name,___ when you're strange,__

when you're strange, ... when you're

strange._____ Al - right,___ yeah.___

RIDERS ON THE STORM

Words and Music by
THE DOORS

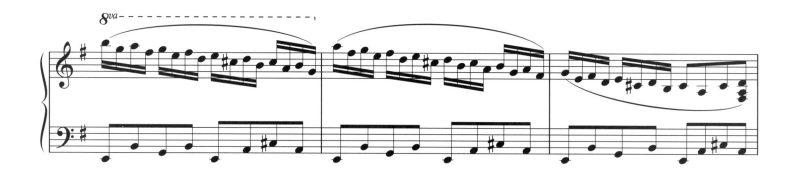

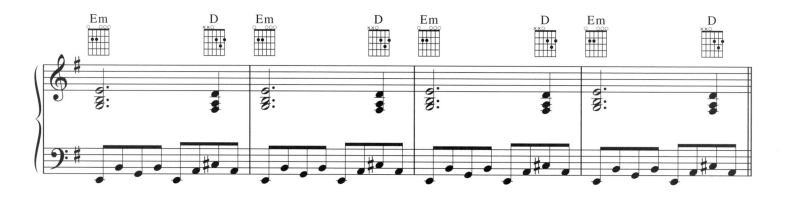

Riders on the Storm - 12 - 1

Verse 1:

180

Verse 2:

Verse 3:

Electric piano solo:

184

188

SOUL KITCHEN

Words and Music by
THE DOORS

Moderately ♩ = 108

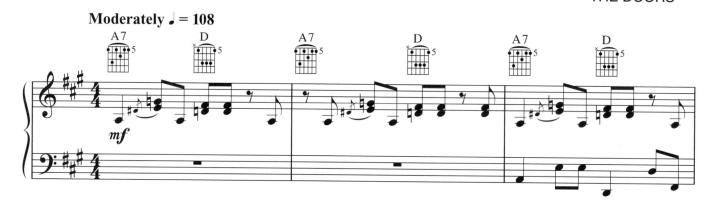

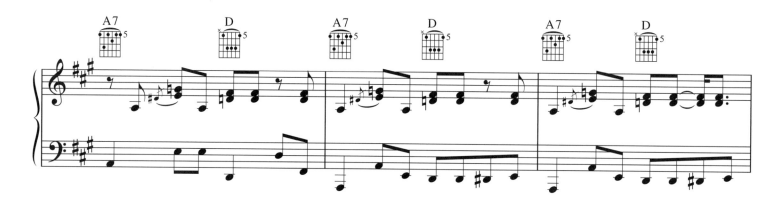

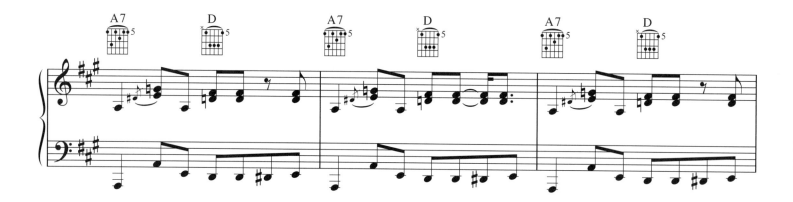

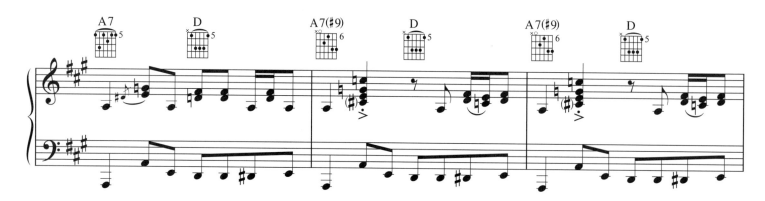

Soul Kitchen - 8 - 1

196

SPANISH CARAVAN

Words and Music by
THE DOORS

Ad lib. Flamenco style

(with pedal)

Moderately bright ♩ = 120

Verse 1:

1. Car - ry me, car - a - van, take me a - way.

a tempo

202

Verse 2:

2. Trade winds find Gal-li-ans lost in the sea.

I know a trea-sure is wait-ing for me.

TELL ALL THE PEOPLE

Words and Music by
ROBBIE KRIEGER

Moderate rock ♩ = 86

(with pedal)

Tell all the peo-ple that__ you see   fol - low

Tell All the People - 7 - 1

Tell All the People - 7 - 4

STRANGE DAYS

Words and Music by
THE DOORS

Moderately ♩ = 128

TOUCH ME

Words and Music by
THE DOORS

Moderately ♩ = 116

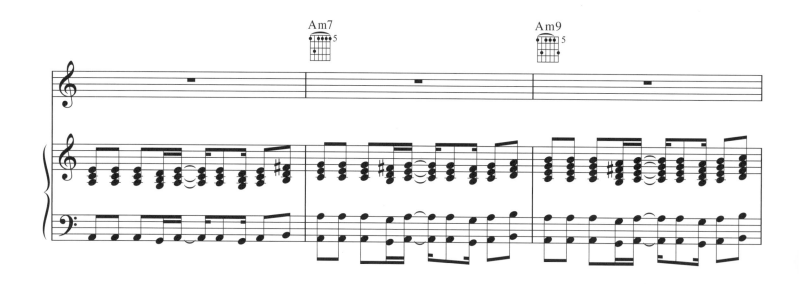

1. Come on,__ come on, come on, come on now

Touch Me - 5 - 1

stars fall from the sky for you and I.

Sax solo:

Play 7 times

WAITING FOR THE SUN

Words and Music by
JIM MORRISON

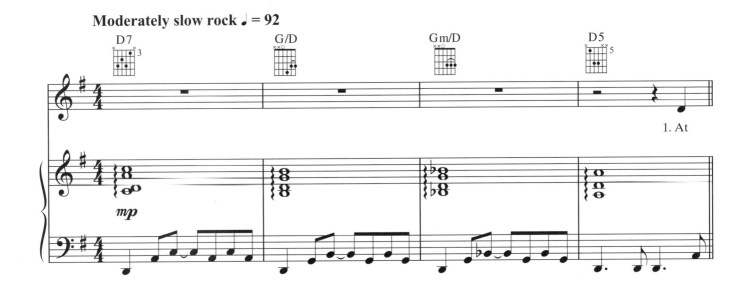

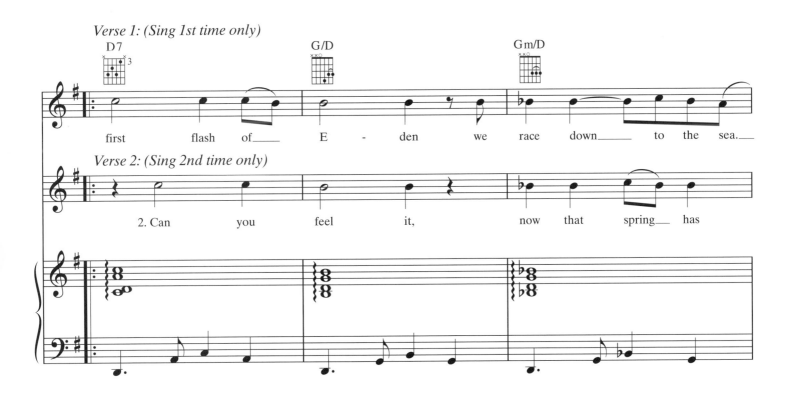

Verse 3:

3. Can you feel it now that spring has come?

That it's time to live in the

TWENTIETH CENTURY FOX

Words and Music by
THE DOORS

Moderate rock ♩ = 116

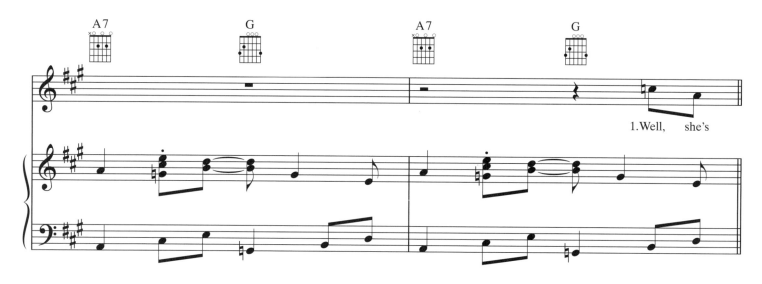

1.Well, she's

𝄋 *Verse:*

fash-ion-a-bly lean,___
queen of cool,___

and she's fash-ion-a-bly late.___
and she's the la-dy___ who waits.___

Twentieth Century Fox - 4 - 1

THE UNKNOWN SOLDIER

Words and Music by
THE DOORS

Freely

Wait un-til the war is o - ver and we're both a lit-tle

old - er. The un-known sol - dier.

Moderate rock ♩ = 120

Verse:

1. Break-fast where the news___ is read,___ tel - e - vi - sion

ver   for the   un-known   sol - dier,   uh,

uh._____

Military drum

"Hup, hup, hup ho he hup.   Hup, hup, hup ho he hup."   "Company....

halt!"   *"Present arms!"*

(Military drum roll/ Gun shot)

Repeat ad lib. and fade

THE WASP
(Texas Radio and the Big Beat)

Words and Music by
THE DOORS

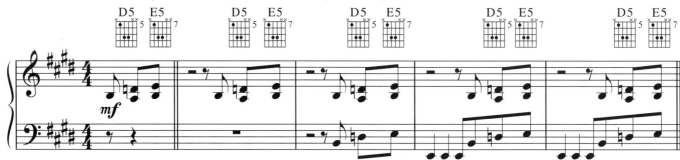

Spoken:
I wanna tell you 'bout Texas Radio and the Big Beat.
Comes out of the Virginia swamps,
Cool and slow with plenty of precision,
With a back beat narrow and hard to master.

Some call it heavenly in its brilliance,
Others, mean and rueful of the Western dream.
I love the friends I have gathered together on this thin raft.
We have constructed pyramids in honor of our escaping.
This is the land where the Pharaoh died.

Play 5 times

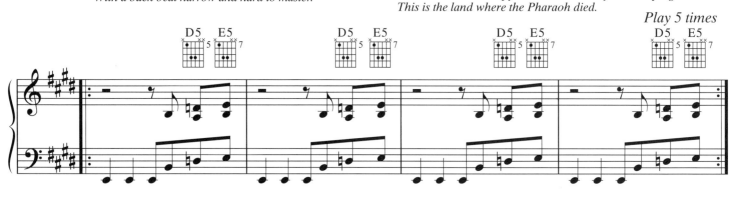

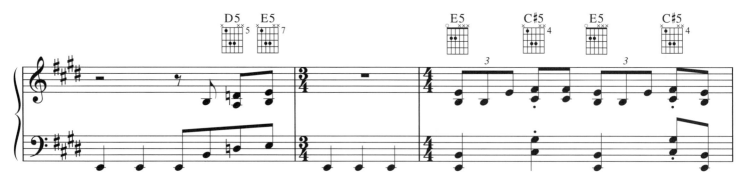

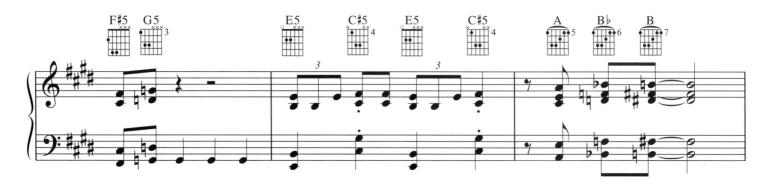

The WASP - 7 - 1

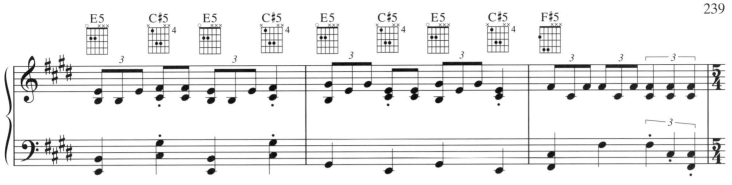

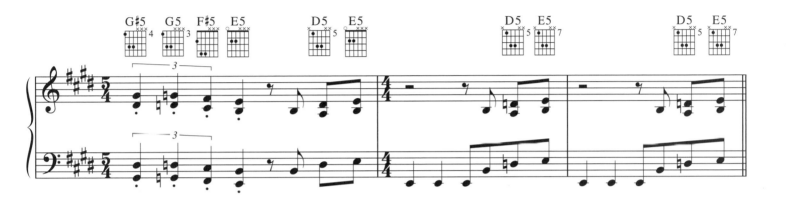

Spoken:
The Negroes in the forest, brightly feathered...
They are saying, "Forget the night.
Live with us in forests of azure.
Out here on the perimeter there are no stars.
Out here we is stoned - immaculate."

Play 2 times

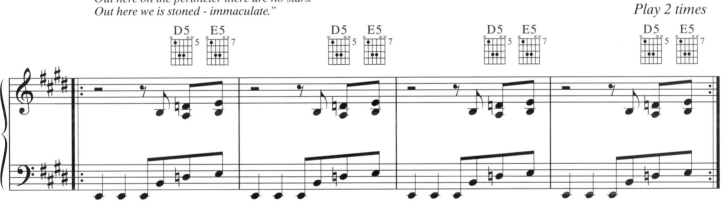

Chorus:

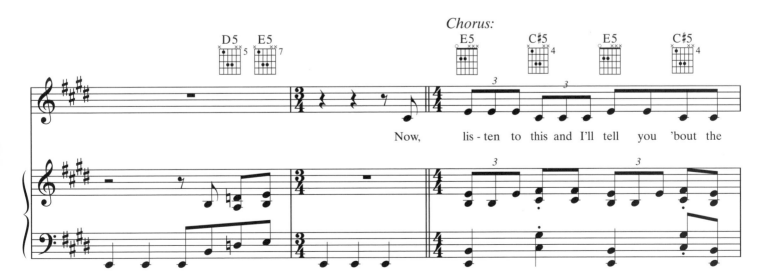

Now,   lis - ten to this and I'll tell   you 'bout the

The WASP - 7 - 2

Spoken:
I'll tell you this... No eternal reward will forgive us now for wasting the dawn.

Spoken: *I'll tell you 'bout Texas Radio and the Big Beat. Soft-driven, slow and mad, like some new language.*

Organ solo:

The WASP - 7 - 6

244

Chorus:

lis-ten to this and I'll tell you 'bout the Tex - as,   I'll   tell you a-bout the Tex   -   as,___

ra - di - o.___   I'll   tell you 'bout the hope-less night,   wan-der-ing the west-ern dream.

tell   you   'bout   the   maid - en   with   wrought   i - ron   soul.

WISHFUL SINFUL

Words and Music by
ROBBY KRIEGER

WHEN THE MUSIC'S OVER

Words and Music by
THE DOORS

When the Music's Over - 16 - 2

Verses 1, 2 & 7:

mu - sic's o - ver...

When the mu - sic's o - ver, yeah...

When the mu - sic's o - ver,

1.2.7. When the

Lyrics under the staves:

girl in the win-dow won't drop.__ A feast of friends,__ "A-

live!," she cried,__ wait-in' for me__ out - side!_____

4. Be -

Verse 4:

Verse 5:

5. Come back,__ ba - by, back in - to my arm.____

We're get - tin' tired__ of hang - in' a - round,___

wait - in' a - round__ with our heads to the ground.__

We want the world and we want it now....   want it...
                        We want the world and we

Now,   now?_____

Organ solo:

Em   A   Em   A   Em   A

Now!_____

mf

Em   A   Em   A   Em   A

Save us!